THE SIMPLIFY DAY

How Entrepreneurs Focus to Achieve Breakthrough Results

Published by
Influential Advisor Media

DISCLAIMER:
This book contains the opinions and ideas of the author and is intended for educational and informational purposes only. Careful attention has been paid to ensure the accuracy of the information presented, but the author cannot assume responsibility for the validity or consequences of its use.

The content of this book should not be construed as specific financial, investment, tax, or legal advice. Every individual's financial situation is unique, and readers should consult with qualified professionals who can evaluate their specific circumstances, needs, and goals before making any financial decisions.

The examples, case studies, and scenarios presented in this book are for illustrative purposes only and do not guarantee or predict any particular outcome. Past performance is not indicative of future results. Individual results will vary.

No reader should act or refrain from acting based solely on the information contained in this book without first seeking appropriate professional advice. Any use of the information found in this book is the sole responsibility of the reader. The author, publisher, and any affiliated entities disclaim any liability for actions taken or not taken based on the contents of this book.

John Vance, CFP®

THE SIMPLIFY DAY

How Entrepreneurs Focus to Achieve Breakthrough Results

INFLUENTIAL
ADVISOR
MEDIA

CONTENTS

INTRODUCTION

I've always been in leadership roles. Quarterback in high school, captain of football and soccer teams. People used to call me "the director." But running a business turned out to be completely different from any leadership role I'd experienced before. No playbook, limited budget, and the direction of the firm wasn't always clear.

When I graduated from Santa Clara University in 1997 with a finance and economics degree, I thought I knew where I was headed. First, though, I took off backpacking through Europe for forty-five days with a buddy, then another couple weeks on a roadtrip around the US. I came back right before Labor Day without a job lined up. So, my mom walked into my room, threw down the Sunday *Los Angeles Times* on my bed, and said, "Alright, time to get a job."

Those were different times. I had interviews within a week and started as a broker trainee within three weeks at a small mom-and-pop firm in Beverly Hills. I spent five years there developing my skills and learning the business. I probably would've stayed longer if my mentor, who'd run his previous firm for more than ten years, hadn't turned out to be doing some dishonest things. When that became clear, I decided to leave. But the timing was actually perfect. It pushed me to take the leap I might not have taken otherwise.

By early 2003, we were coming out of the dot-com crash, and I had a decision to make. It was a scary time economically, and starting a business felt risky. But I remembered all the articles I read about how some of the greatest American companies were founded during hard times. So I thought, *"If I'm going to take the leap, why not now?"*

I launched my business a month before my first daughter was born. My wife at the time had just quit her journalism job to stay home with the baby, so we were going from two incomes to zero income. I was starting completely from scratch. We had maybe six months of reserves, and that first year was pretty hard.

I was twenty-eight and, at that age, you feel fearless. But the truth is, I had a lot to lose. We were just starting a family, and we had no safety net. That responsibility of having a newborn, knowing people were depending on me was my driving force. If I'd been single, I don't think I would've pushed nearly as hard. There's something about being relied on that sharpens your focus.

What I learned is that starting from zero forces you to figure things out fast. The hardest part wasn't what I expected. I had five years of experience, so I understood the basics of financial planning strategies and many ways to advise clients. But how do you *get* those clients?

I knew I wasn't naturally sales-minded, but I was a teacher at heart. So I found my way into eight different community colleges throughout Southern California, teaching night classes on everything from financial planning to starting investment clubs. When you have to teach something, you learn it at a completely different level. And more importantly, it put me in front of people who eventually became my first clients.

I still have some of those original clients today, and I sometimes joke with them, "What were you thinking, hiring me at that age?" My knowledge back then, compared to where it is today, was obviously very novice. But they always say the same thing.

"We trusted you. We knew you'd do what you said you were going to do."

Going back to my teaching days, I can see the value of that experience for my business. When you teach, you're not trying to sell anyone on anything. You're trying to give them a clear understanding about the landscape, whether it's around core financial planning disciplines or investment strategies.

That experience taught me to approach conversations with a teacher's mindset. And in my experience, two things might happen when you do that. First, people realize what we do is actually pretty complicated. They see there's a level of complexity they hadn't appreciated before, and many of them don't want to handle it themselves; they'd rather work with someone who can guide them through it. And second, when you communicate like a teacher, people don't feel talked-down to or sold to.

That became the foundation of everything we built. We focus on having engaging conversations, asking thoughtful questions, uncovering real challenges and pain points, and then building solutions around those needs.

But it hasn't always been this way. When you're starting a business, gaining a customer takes enormous effort, so you do whatever it takes to keep that trust. Do what you say you're going to do, follow up diligently, and when you make a mistake, own it and fix it.

Those early years were a grind. Starting at $75,000, then $200,000, then $350,000 revenue . . . just slowly building.

At the beginning, I was doing everything myself, including answering phones, taking out the trash, scanning papers, and filling out forms. Now we've got a team of over twenty-five and growing. It's exciting when I think back to where it all started.

THE REALITY NOBODY WARNS YOU ABOUT

Nobody tells you that growth doesn't just bring opportunity. It may also bring complexity.

At the beginning, everything got done exactly the way I wanted because I was the one doing it. But as revenue grew, and I added employees, complexity showed up almost overnight. Suddenly, I wasn't just getting new clients. I had to manage people, build systems, and make sure clients weren't just onboarded but consistently served well.

And if you're an entrepreneur reading this, whether you're just starting out or years into building something, you probably know exactly what I'm talking about.

When you're starting a business, there's no choice but to wear all the hats. You do sales and marketing, service delivery, and client management. You handle all of it whether you're good at it or not. In those early stages, you're in survival mode, struggling just to get it done. And as you're limited with resources, that becomes almost a natural path. You start with the basics of your team, building it out of necessity as you go.

The benefit of that is that you learn every nuance of your business. But as your business grows, complexity comes in, and you suddenly recognize the downside that you're doing things that are not your natural strengths. You've built something successful, but there's this sense that something's still missing. If this sounds familiar, you're the one I wrote this book for.

As you're starting your business (and even as you begin to experience some success), you're often working at a frenetic, busy pace that likely lacks a lot of focus. It's the classic "ready, fire, aim" scenario. You just have to go because you can't wait for things to be perfect.

Have you ever heard the saying, "Perfection is the enemy of success"? That's true. Some businesses fail simply because the owner is so focused on making everything perfect that they never launch. On the other hand, you have business owners who are great at making decisions and moving quickly, so they *do* launch. But the frenetic pace never leaves them. They end up living in a constant state of chaos without any real sense of normalcy.

As you break through those early phases, you achieve a level of success where you're beyond the startup stage. You're not worried about putting food on the table anymore. You've moved past that foundational level where you're just trying to cover your basic needs. And when you get beyond that, you can finally afford to be more purposeful with your decision making.

Issues that weren't even on your radar before, like income taxes, which hadn't been a big concern when you weren't earning much, are now very real. You're at a point where you want to be more intentional and more organized, making the kinds of decisions that will set you up to build long-term wealth.

In this book, I'll introduce you to a framework built around a simple idea. I call it The Simplify Day, a monthly planning day designed to create space to work on your business instead of in it. It's designed to help you shift from reactive to proactive, from firefighting to measuring success.

In the pages ahead, I'll walk you through how this works at different stages of the entrepreneurial journey.

We'll start by focusing on the fundamentals that every entrepreneur needs, regardless of where you are. In this first part, we'll explore the common challenges entrepreneurs face, how to plan and run your first Simplify Day, and key strategies you can apply whether you're just starting out or already have years of experience.

Then we'll address what can happen as your business grows and complexity increases. We'll cover how to build systems, so your team of professionals can work together without you having to manage everything. And I'll share ideas for creating a planning structure that can help you balance your business with the rest of your life.

But most importantly, we'll explore a path that can lead from complexity to freedom. Not just financial freedom, but freedom of time, energy, and clarity. It's about bringing the three circles of self, family, and business into harmony, so success finally gives you what you wanted all along.

PART ONE

BUILDING THE FRAMEWORK

TO MOVE FROM COMPLEXITY to freedom, we need a strong foundation. And this foundation starts with understanding the pain points you're already experiencing, like feeling like you're constantly putting out fires instead of working on your business with no white space to think strategically.

So in this first section, we'll dedicate the next three chapters to look at why this happens, introduce the monthly planning system that changed everything for me, and cover a tax strategy that can work at any stage.

CHAPTER 1:

THE CHALLENGES OF SUCCESS

AS ENTREPRENEURS START SEEING some success, and they're finally past the true startup phase (survival-mode stage), they naturally begin shifting their mindset. Instead of thinking only about keeping the business alive, they start asking, "How do I optimize what I'm doing?" and "How do I make sure the decisions I'm making are actually the best ones?" Because for a long time, the entire focus has been on moving the business forward, and that focus tends to stay centered on the day-to-day work.

Besides, while you were focused on growing, you were also accumulating professionals, adding them as problems came up. Now you're managing all these outside advisors and wondering whether they're working together, or if you've built a piecemeal team that adds complexity instead of solving it.

So, as you've made it past that first phase, it can be hard to build the habits you need to get more focused and truly optimize what you've built. In that stage, you might recognize some pain points:

- You feel like you've plateaued, even though revenue is decent
- You're spending too much time coordinating your team of professionals instead of growing your business
- You hate wasting money and paying too much in taxes after working so hard to get here
- The question shifts from, "Will my business survive?" to, "Am I doing this right?"
- You've realized what got you here won't get you to the next level

Running a business comes with challenges that can slowly wear you down. You're constantly busy, putting out fires and struggling to find time for the strategic work that moves the business forward. As you become more successful, a siloed team of professionals can feel like juggling too many balls at once, especially when no one is truly communicating.

On top of that, tax and financial planning can become major sources of stress. All of this leaves you feeling overwhelmed and unsure how to get back in control.

To illustrate how this can happen, consider this hypothetical scenario. A business owner set up a retirement plan several years ago based on advice from a professional they trusted at the time. The plan was designed to help them save on taxes, and initially, it may have done exactly that.

Over the years, the business grew significantly with more employees, more revenue, and more complexity, but nobody revisited the plan to make sure it still made sense. The retirement plan, which once benefited the owner, gradually shifted. More employees meant more contributions the owner had to make on behalf of the broader team, and at a certain point, they were putting in far more to cover everyone else than they were getting back in personal tax savings. Nobody caught that issue.

That's where a lot of entrepreneurs can find themselves. You get advice to do something, and maybe it's the right move at the time. But if no one is revisiting it year after year, that advice can become outdated. The tax code changes, income goes up, the dynamics of the business change. What made sense before doesn't necessarily make sense now.

In a situation like this, the business owner might want to simplify things, but unwinding what was set up years ago can be complicated and expensive.

And often, the hardest part isn't the financial impact itself; it's the realization that nobody asked the tough questions upfront. What do we want to accomplish? How long are we doing this? What happens as we grow? Will this still work in five years?

This kind of scenario can also create hesitancy. When business owners feel they've been let down by their professional team before, it can be difficult to trust that the next advisor will be any different. That's just how entrepreneurs are wired. We believe in results, not promises.

This chapter breaks down why even smart, successful entrepreneurs end up in situations like this. How professional teams get built piecemeal out of necessity rather than strategy. Why having multiple smart professionals doesn't mean having integrated solutions. And most importantly, why entrepreneurs stay stuck even when they know something's wrong, and what it takes to finally break free.

THE PIECEMEAL PROFESSIONAL TEAM

Many entrepreneurs tend to build their professional team without a clear strategy. As we discussed, during the early stages of your business you're more likely to focus on growth, serving clients, and keeping your business working. So, you do what every entrepreneur does. You solve problems as they come up.

For example, when you start a business, the first thing you need is an attorney to set up your entity. Then, an accountant for taxes, an insurance agent for coverage, maybe a book keeper, and so on . . . you find them mostly through referrals or just whoever seems affordable at the time. You add them to your team and let them do the job you hired them for.

But then you look up, and you might have five to ten professionals working for you. To get the most out of your team, they need to be actively collaborating to serve you. The problem is, there's usually no mechanism for that. So you end up being the one in the middle, coordinating communication, making sure things are optimized, and driving the collaboration.

You're trying to be smart about costs. You don't want to waste money having professionals collaborate on things that aren't relevant, and you know how expensive some of these professionals can be. So you make yourself the coordinator, acting as a quarterback between all these professionals. You become the middleman who connects all the dots.

The problem is that you've hired these professionals to delegate work to experts and free up your time, so you could focus on growing your business and achieving your personal goals. Instead, that time is now spent managing the very people who were supposed to give it back to you.

So, you end up doing a job you've never been trained for. You don't know when the work overlaps, you don't know which professionals should be talking to each other and when, and you don't fully comprehend what it takes to manage a team like this effectively.

This approach can create gaps, overlaps, and blind spots you may not even realize are there.

This trial and error cycle is part of what creates that mess. After all, you're learning as you go while trying to run and grow your business at the same time.

Besides, it's harder to think strategically about assembling an integrated professional team when you're limited with resources. So, many entrepreneurs feel tempted to figure it out themselves, thinking they'll save money. And this temptation is even worse today with AI tools that might give you reasonable answers but don't have a deep understanding of your specific situation. So, you just *hope* they're right.

As your business grows, success brings more complexity. It becomes clear that you're managing a set of professionals who know their job really well but don't necessarily work together, and that makes you feel frustrated.

Sometimes you may outgrow your professionals, too. The CPA who was perfect when you were smaller may no longer have the expertise you need now. But by then, you've got history, relationships, and maybe even friendship. Making changes can feel disruptive and risky, so you keep these professionals that no longer serve you.

SMART PROFESSIONALS VS. INTEGRATED SOLUTIONS

At this point, you might be thinking, "Sure, I built my team out of necessity, but they're all smart professionals. How could that possibly lead to gaps or missed opportunities?"

There's a big difference between having multiple smart professionals and having them work as an integrated solution.

Smart professionals are essential. You want advisors who are highly trained, competent, and experts in their lane. That's what most business owners end up with specialists who are each very good at what they do.

But the problem is that, oftentimes, those professionals operate in silos. The CPA looks only at taxes, the attorney only at legal structures, and the insurance agent only at policies. Each decision might make sense in isolation, but no one checks whether all the pieces work together.

An integrated solution looks different. With someone in the quarterback seat, the business owner still makes the big decisions, but they no longer manage the team. The quarterback ensures the team is aligned, communication is clear, and every professional's work connects back to the business owner's overall goals.

One of the benefits of having smart professionals is that there can be disagreement. Full alignment isn't realistic, nor is it even desirable. The tension between different perspectives often leads to better decisions. Your CPA might want to minimize this year's taxes while your financial advisor is thinking about long-term wealth building. That tension is valuable.

Without someone at the center to facilitate and integrate, the tension can turn into conflict or paralysis. With the right coordination, it can turn into synergy. And in my experience, synergy tends to produce better outcomes.

THE EMOTIONAL AND PRACTICAL COST

The dominant emotion I see when successful entrepreneurs realize they're spending time managing their professional team is frustration. Entrepreneurs thrive when they're operating in their area of expertise, building, creating, and leading. But when they're forced to manage financial, legal, and administrative details they're not trained for, it pulls them out of their zone and drains their energy.

Running a business can feel like constant chaos. You feel like you're always reacting, never really getting ahead. And when you finally try to focus, everything stalls. Projects get delayed, documents sit untouched, and decisions hang because someone else hasn't completed their task.

Both the urgency and the delays are symptoms of the same problem . . . a reactive professional team without anyone setting the agenda and driving the process proactively.

Running a business is demanding enough, but when you layer on coordinating multiple professionals, tracking loose ends, and bridging the gap between business and personal finances, it becomes a massive distraction. Where do entrepreneurs *want* to spend their energy?

- Taking care of themselves: health, exercise, family time, personal growth

- Serving their customers or patients: the work they're passionate about

- Supporting their employees: building culture, developing talent, creating opportunities

Instead, they're stuck in the middle of this professional team mess, coordinating people and strategies they don't fully understand.

And I understand that feeling completely. Even though I know how to do all this coordination, I don't want to run my own stuff, either. I have someone on my team who helps me because I want to spend my time serving clients, growing the business, and being present for my family. Nobody builds a successful business because they love managing administrative complexity.

THE PATH FORWARD

You've built a successful business because you're excellent at serving customers and solving problems in your area of expertise. But now you feel like you're spending too much energy on coordination and administration instead of the strategic thinking that actually drives growth.

When you're stuck managing the people you hired to free you up, you haven't solved the problem. You've just made it more expensive. But this isn't about replacing your team or overhauling everything overnight. It's about creating a system that gives you back control, not by working harder or hiring more people, but by building the discipline to work on your business instead of just in it. And that starts with carving out dedicated time to think.

CHAPTER 2:

THE SIMPLIFY DAY CONCEPT AND SET UP - YOUR PATH TO STRATEGIC PLANNING

ONE OF THE BIGGEST value-adds for business owners is the ability to set clear goals and then consistently measure progress against them. When you think about strategic planning, that's really the foundation. Planning begins with defining what you want to achieve.

But something that matters as much as setting those goals is building systems that force you to pause, check in, and honestly assess where things stand. Every business needs a structured way to set goals and a reliable process for reviewing performance on a regular basis.

That's where the Simplify Day fits in. It becomes a built-in monthly checkpoint (roughly every thirty days) where you step back, evaluate your results, and realign your actions.

It's a simple rhythm that can keep you grounded, focused, and moving forward.

Although I've been on this entrepreneurial journey for over twenty years, Simplify Day, as it is today, has only really existed for about four years. It's been a gradual process of slow building and refining.

I've always had a decent habit for self-reflecting over short periods of time; nothing formal, just checking back in to assess what was happening.

In the beginning, I had to build my own self-discipline around whatever mattered most. When you're starting a business, you're doing so much on your own and carrying so many responsibilities that developing discipline becomes essential, especially in the areas you struggle with. If you don't strengthen those weak spots, that's often where the business starts to run into trouble. So, as a small business owner, I had no choice but to be disciplined. But as my team started to grow and we had more financial success, I started getting away from those basic disciplines that got me that far. We'd grown from eight employees to twenty-five. Revenue climbed from $2 million to $6.4 million. And I noticed that my performance wasn't as good as it needed to be.

I had limited white space to do the deep work around projects. Oftentimes, I was just dealing with putting out fires and focusing on urgencies. You know how it goes. You start the day determined to finally get something meaningful done, and then the fires start. By the end of the day, you're exhausted and thinking, "I didn't get to it again." That cycle repeats, and it eats away at you.

Although I love solving problems (I'm a business owner, right? That's what I love doing), those urges got all my attention, and because of that, it got really hard to start or complete the projects that had more complexity. When you're in that situation, you feel mentally drained because you *know* those things were important, but you never seem to make real progress.

So, one day, I read about Bill Gates' ideas around "think weeks," a time when he'd completely disconnect and head off to a cabin somewhere in the Pacific Northwest. He'd spend days there reading, thinking, and doing deep work completely away from the noise of everyday life and the office.

I thought, "That's exactly what I need." So I tried it with three-day blocks, three times a year. Sometimes offsite, sometimes at a local hotel.

But my first attempt at day one wasn't as I expected. I sat there with all my saved articles and books thinking, "How am I going to fill all this time?" I'd read for hours but couldn't get into any real action mode. I was just consuming content with no clear direction.

Now, day two was highly effective. I started to roadmap projects and connect ideas I'd been gathering for months about things like our client onboarding process. But on day three, I was completely out of energy. I just felt like, "Okay, I got nothing left."

I tried this a few more times. Same pattern every time. I had one productive day between two mediocre ones. Plus, three nights away from my wife Carmen and our kids was a lot to ask. And sometimes four months would pass between these mini-retreats. The problems I needed to solve couldn't wait that long.

So I started thinking, *"What if I could get that same focus in just one day per month?"*

This is what we're going to discuss in this chapter. I'll show you exactly how Simplify Day works, from the morning routine that sets the tone, to the thirty-day review that keeps you accountable, to identifying the three big issues worth your focused time. Most importantly, you'll understand why this is beyond time management. You need space for the work that moves your business forward.

THE CORE STRUCTURE

My Simplify Day starts at 5 a.m. Not because 5 a.m. is magic but because that's when the house is quiet, and I can set the tone for the day.

I usually start by reading for about an hour. Sometimes it's a new book that sparks ideas. Other times it's a classic I come back to every few years. No email, no screens, just reading. This shifts my brain into a creative mode. It gives me space to process, reflect, and begin thinking about the issues I want to tackle.

That's important because, as we'll explore later, most Simplify Days are structured around two or three big issues, each requiring two to three hours of deep work. By starting with reading, I prime myself to do that work with clarity and focus instead of immediately responding to other people's priorities.

After reading, I'll do a light workout. Nothing intense, just enough to get the energy flowing. By the time I'm done, I'm ready for the real work.

THE THIRTY-DAY REVIEW

Every Simplify Day starts by setting clear objectives and reviewing the last thirty days. But this really begins weeks beforehand.

Throughout the month, I journal and jot down two or three projects (or issues) I know I'll need to work on. Here, we're not thinking about urgent items because those issues will always find you. They're priorities that need to be scheduled, or they'll get crowded out by daily fires.

I've built a "parking lot" that is a digital file where I store links, articles, and ideas. My team can even drop stuff in there. By the time my Simplify Day comes around, I'm not scrambling to figure out what to work on. I already know what matters most.

The review itself is straightforward. What were my goals for the last thirty days? How did I do? I grade myself, refine where needed, and recommit to the next thirty days. That cycle of review and reset keeps me accountable.

This is where Dan Sullivan's concept of *The Gap and The Gain* comes in. Most entrepreneurs measure themselves against the horizon or the gap between where they are and where they want to be. That's exhausting. You never arrive. And even if you do, you push the goal out further.

The Simplify Day reframes this. By reviewing what I set out to do in the last thirty days, I can see the progress, however small. Living in the gain means acknowledging and building on forward movement instead of beating yourself up for not being "there" yet.

The beauty of thirty-day cycles is you get to start fresh. If you wait a whole year to review your goals and you had a bad year, that's a lot of wasted time. Thirty days you can recover from.

THREE MAIN ISSUES

After the review, I tackle three main issues. These come straight from the parking lot I've been building all month with the projects and problems I've been journaling about that need dedicated focus. I prioritize them in order because sometimes one takes the entire day.

Each issue gets a two-hour block. During those blocks, there is no email, no Teams, no phone, no multitasking. Just focused attention on that single issue. Two hours is long enough to make real progress but short enough to maintain sharp focus.

I was amazed, early on, that things I thought would take six hours because I'd been starting and stopping for weeks got done in two hours of focused time. We build up these tasks in our minds, but when you eliminate interruptions and just do the work, it goes faster than you think. This is Parkinson's Law in action. Work expands to fill the time available for its completion.

Let me give you a concrete example. This past year, we added three new partners to Vance Wealth, which meant redoing our entire operating agreement. Sixty pages of legal documents that needed review, revision, and careful attention to every detail.

For weeks, I'd been trying to tackle it in bits and pieces. I'd sit down, read through a section for an hour, then get pulled into a client call or a team issue. The next time I picked it up, I'd have to reread what I'd already covered just to get back into the right mindset. That start-stop pattern is a terrible use of time, and I knew it. But the document was dense, technical, and, honestly, not the kind of work I enjoy. So it kept getting pushed aside.

Finally, I dedicated an entire Simplify Day to it. No interruptions, no distractions, just me and those sixty pages. I moved through the document section by section, making notes, flagging issues, working through the language with the level of focus that kind of work demands.

The work wasn't fun. I remember thinking, *"Thankfully I'm not an attorney, because that was painful."* But the reality is that once I set aside dedicated time to focus on that work, it became much easier than I expected. It got done, and it got done right. What I'd been dragging out for months, picking it up and putting it down without real progress, I finished in one focused day.

I thought it would take forever, but once I set aside a full day and cut out distractions, I powered through it.

Some Simplify Days can run fourteen hours long. It seems a lot, I know, but when they're structured right, they're energizing, not exhausting. There's something about making real progress on important work that gives you energy instead of draining it.

WHEN HOME DOESN'T WORK

Your personal residence is the ideal setting for Simplify Days. But sometimes home just isn't the right environment. You might have young kids who need attention, construction happening next door, or general distractions that make focus impossible. You need to know your environment and be honest about what will work.

So, if home isn't viable, one effective option is to book a hotel for two nights. Check in the afternoon before, settle in, enjoy a good meal, and get a full night's rest. The next day, you'll have uninterrupted time for deep, focused work, with room service and all the amenities to support you.

Checking out the following morning allows you to wrap up calmly and transition back without rushing. The two-night stay also provides a useful comparable for fair market value when applying the Augusta Rule, which we'll explore in the next chapter.

Another option for entrepreneurs who prefer to stay home is what I like to call the "Family Buy-In." Send everyone off with a little money to do something fun. Okay, I'll admit, that part's mostly for fun. But the idea behind it is absolutely true, and I'll share a personal example to show you what I mean.

During the summer, when the kids are home, I often encourage my wife, Carmen, and the kids to spend the day doing something they enjoy, like shopping, getting outside, or having their own little adventure. That way, I can focus fully, and they don't feel like my Simplify Day is taking anything away from them.

I've explained how this day helps me stay focused, present, and ultimately better for both the business and our family. And once they understand, they respect the boundaries I set.

While I call it a "day," it's not as if I'm locked in my home office for twelve straight hours. I move around the house. I use the office, the kitchen, the living room, the patio for fresh air and natural light, or even the gym. My Simplify Day has become part of the rhythm of our home life, and because my family sees the value in it, they support it rather than view it as a sacrifice.

BUILDING YOUR KNOWLEDGE LIBRARY

My dad was a public speaker, and growing up, I'd see stacks of yellow legal pads around the house. That was his system. Write everything out by hand, process ideas on paper. I picked up that habit. For twenty years, I filled journals and notebooks the same way.

The problem showed up when I needed to find something. If I wanted to remember what I'd written about a specific topic three years ago, I had to dig through old pages. The ideas were valuable, but they were effectively buried. I'd rarely go back to them because the friction was too high.

That changed when I started digitizing everything. Now, throughout the month, I do what I call a "data dump." Journaling, saving articles, and capturing ideas . . . I feed it all into ChatGPT projects without worrying about making it perfect or organized. Just get it in there.

What that means practically is that when my Simplify Day comes around, I can pull up two decades of notes instantly. I can search for themes, ask questions, and connect ideas I'd completely forgotten about. Instead of starting from scratch every time I work on a problem, I'm building on work I've already done. The AI acts like a thought partner. It helps me organize ideas and spot patterns I might have missed.

I've been part of Vistage for over eight years with monthly peer group meetings where you're learning from other business owners, getting exposed to new ideas. Before I paired it with Simplify Days, I'd walk away with a notebook full of insights and never look at them again. Now I schedule my Simplify Day right after Vistage. I do a full debrief and consider what applies to our business and what can be discarded. That single change took Vistage from theoretical learning to actual business execution.

The shortcut here is simple:

- Start capturing your notes digitally now
- Pick an AI tool and feed everything into it
- Don't organize it, don't make it pretty, just capture it

Over time, you build your own searchable library that makes every Simplify Day more effective. This allows you to have your best thinking available exactly when you need it.

WHAT CLIENTS DISCOVER

Most of the stress and inefficiency we feel as entrepreneurs isn't because the work is too hard; it's because we may not give ourselves the space to actually *do* it. Realizing that was my biggest "aha" moment. It sounds simple, but when you're fully engaged in one activity without noise or interruptions, your effectiveness skyrockets.

For example, imagine you're a business owner managing a growing team, say, more than a dozen employees, and someone introduces you to the Simplify Day concept. Your first reaction could probably be, "I'm too busy to take a full day away from operations."

But after seeing how the structure could work, you decide to give it a try. The setup is straightforward with sample agendas and calendar reminders to provide the framework. But you're the one doing the actual work. Over the following months, you may start noticing shifts in how you manage your time and priorities. Maybe you started identifying inefficiencies and making more intentional decisions. Over time, that kind of consistent, focused effort could contribute to real improvements in both profitability and income.

Of course, many factors influence business growth. But the potential downstream impact of giving yourself dedicated time to work *on* your business rather than just *in* it is the real value of this practice.

START WHERE YOU ARE

The Simplify Day isn't one-size-fits-all. Here are three structures to consider:

- **The Beginner's Day**: Focus on goal-setting and light journaling. Pick one or two issues to tackle. This is about building the habit, not overwhelming yourself.

- **The Growth Day:** For entrepreneurs in expansion mode. Deep work on financial planning, team coordination, major business challenges. This is when you're ready to tackle the complex stuff.

- **The Reset Day:** My current structure. Reading in the morning, thirty-day review, then three big issues in two-hour blocks. This is the full system once you've got the rhythm down.

You're probably not going to be great at this right away. My first few Simplify Days felt awkward. Some were amazing, others just okay. That's normal. Give yourself some grace.

What matters is that you start. Pick your day, block it off, tell your family, set up your parking lot for ideas, and commit to stepping out of your business for one day to work on what really matters.

The goal isn't perfection; it's consistency! That important work you keep putting off is not going away. But with a Simplify Day, you finally have a place to get it done.

RESOURCES

Reading suggestions:

Deep Work: Rules for Focused Success in a Distracted World. Newport, C. (2016). Grand Central Publishing.

The Gap And The Gain. Sullivan, D.; Hardy, B. (2021). Hay House Business.

CHAPTER 3:

UNLOCKING THE AUGUSTA RULE - HOW YOUR SIMPLIFY DAY ENABLES TAX SAVINGS

ANYTIME YOU HEAR ABOUT a part of the tax code that allows a business owner to withdraw money from their business in a tax-free manner, it definitely catches your attention. You can't help but think, *"That's interesting! Tell me more about that."*

That was exactly my reaction when I first learned about the Augusta Rule about five years ago, when a tax professional we worked with brought it up during a strategy session with a mutual client. At first glance, it seemed like a small opportunity with potential savings that might range from $5,000 to $10,000 annually. Nice but not exactly game-changing for the clients we work with.

But as we dug deeper, we realized it could be much more substantial, sometimes upwards of $20,000 to $30,000 per year or even more, depending on individual circumstances. That definitely got my attention.

The Augusta Rule, technically IRC Section 280A(g), allows you to rent your personal residence to your business for up to fourteen days per year without paying tax on that rental income. Your business gets the deduction, you receive the income personally, and if done correctly, it's completely tax-free to you.

But what's the legitimate business purpose for renting your home to your business? You could host a team-building event. You could also host leadership meetings at your house. So I started asking myself if this could work if it was just me. Could I rent my house to myself for business purposes? And more importantly, what would I be doing during those days that would hold up under scrutiny?

By that time, I'd already been doing some informal periodic goal reviews on my business and personal progress. Nothing structured, just taking time when I could to assess what was happening. But these check-ins were sporadic, and the important work kept getting pushed aside. That's when I had the idea. What if I formalized this into a dedicated day once a month? One day to step out of the day-to-day and work on the business instead of in it.

That would give me a legitimate business purpose in my monthly planning sessions. Besides, I would finally create the space I needed to do the work that kept falling to the bottom of my list. So, as you already know, that became what we just explored in Chapter 2. But this time, we're looking at it through a different perspective. This is not just a tool for growth and organization, but a smart, legitimate way to potentially benefit from tax savings through the Augusta Rule.

However, documentation is a crucial piece to make this work. And I have an example that shows what can happen when someone tries to apply the Augusta Rule without being properly prepared.

A few years ago, a group of doctors tried to use an aggressive application of the Augusta Rule to save on taxes[1]. When the IRS reviewed their case, everything quickly fell apart. The doctors had no documentation, and some of the dates they claimed didn't even correspond to any business activity. They had essentially made it all up.

The IRS disallowed nearly all of the deductions. When the case went to the tax court, the judges allowed only $500 for four specific days where there was at least some documentation showing that work had been done. The rest was completely thrown out.

Now, most people look at this case and say, "See? The Augusta Rule doesn't work. It's too risky." But I saw it differently. The court actually validated that there is an allowable amount *when you do it right*. The issue wasn't the strategy itself but *how it was applied*. They didn't have a clear business purpose, documentation, or legitimate structure.

What we'll discuss in this chapter is how to use the Augusta Rule the right way, how the Simplify Day framework

---

1 Zollars, E. (2023, August 16). Current Federal Tax Developments. Current Federal Tax Developments. https://www.currentfederaltaxdevelopments.com/blog/2023/8/15/tax-court-greatly-reduces-rent-deduction-for-s-corporation-where-taxpayer-attempted-to-take-advantage-of-the-masters-rule

may help you take advantage of this potential benefit, who may qualify, how to establish legitimate business purpose, what documentation you need, and most importantly, how this tax strategy could positively impact the way you run your business.

WHO QUALIFIES

When I first heard about the Augusta Rule, I started asking myself if I could rent my house to myself for business purposes. Who qualifies?

Well, to qualify for the Augusta Rule, the most important thing is that your home cannot be your primary place of work. If you're working from home 100 or 200 days a year, you can't then rent it to yourself for another fourteen days.

As we discussed, the Augusta Rule, by design, is for renting your home to your business for up to fourteen days. When you're already using it as your primary workplace, there's no legitimate business purpose for those additional rental days.

The other key requirement is having a formal business entity. If you're a sole proprietor filing on Schedule C, there's no legal separation between you as an individual and you as the business owner. You're technically the same entity. S-Corps and partnerships tend to be the best vehicle for the Augusta Rule, though C-Corps may work, as well. If you're currently a sole proprietor, you might need to restructure your business entity to qualify.

Your house *cannot* be used for social events with clients. Hosting client dinners or networking parties doesn't qualify. However, hosting team events absolutely works. As an example, every summer, we do a barbecue where we invite our entire team and their families to the house. That counts as one of our rental days. In December, we'll host something at the house for the holidays, like a cocktail party or team dinner, which becomes day two[2].

The other twelve days are my Simplify Days, which are the monthly strategic planning days we discussed in the last chapter. Committing to monthly planning sessions as a business owner covers twelve of the fourteen allowable days. The final two days stay flexible.

Once you understand the framework, you can structure it to match your business needs while staying completely within the rules.

THE FAIR MARKET VALUE CHALLENGE

After learning about the Augusta Rule, establishing fair market value becomes an immediate puzzle to solve. How do you figure out what to charge when renting your home to your business? You need legitimate comparables, but finding them turned out to be trickier than expected.

In my own experience, my first thought was to check VRBO or AirBNB rates. But nobody in my neighborhood was renting their house for just one day. And if you try to estimate by dividing a monthly rental rate by thirty, the number ends up so low it's hardly worth the paperwork.

2 The examples and information in this book are for illustrative purposes only and should not be taken as tax or legal advice. Readers are encouraged to consult qualified tax or legal professionals to evaluate their specific situation.

The breakthrough came from an unexpected source. One of my mentors in Strategic Coach used to talk about her "Ritz Carlton days." I was curious about what that meant. She explained that every quarter, she'd book three or four nights at the Ritz to think, write, and develop content. She needed that time away from the noise to work on thought leadership. Being in a beautiful environment brought out her best thinking. She'd get pampered, have great meals, and maybe hit the spa. It elevated her mood and her energy. That's when it clicked for me.

If you needed to do strategic planning away from your office, what would it cost to create that environment elsewhere? If we consider my mentor's "Ritz Carlton days," here's how it would work:

To get a full day of strategic work at a hotel, you'd need:

- Check in the night before (to wake up fresh and ready)
- A junior suite with proper workspace (not working from a bed)
- A second night (because checking out at noon cuts your productive time in half)

Let's say the Four Seasons or Ritz Carlton in your area runs about $2,000 per night for a junior suite. That's $4,000 comparable for your planning day, a legitimate market rate for creating that working environment.

Based on these comparables, you could land between $2,000 and $4,000 per day. This isn't pushing for the highest possible number; it's establishing a defensible value based on real market data.

Now, this is where some CPAs tend to push back. They'll ask, "How can you justify staying at the Ritz and spending $2,000 a night when you could stay at a Motel 6 for a hundred bucks?

But let me turn the question around. Say a business owner flies from Los Angeles to New York or London for a conference and chooses a lay-flat business-class seat that costs $10,000 round trip. Do you think the IRS would step in and say, "Based on your business, you shouldn't have made that decision. That's too expensive"? Of course not!

The IRS doesn't judge whether you spend money poorly or wisely. That's *your* decision as a business owner. And when it comes to your Simplify Day, it goes back to what we discussed in Chapter 2. Understand your environment and be honest about what truly works for you. If staying at the Ritz creates the proper environment for you to do strategic work that moves your business forward, then that's a legitimate business expense.

The same logic applies to the Augusta Rule. You're not looking for the cheapest option. You're establishing what a legitimate working environment costs and what you'd have to pay if you couldn't use your own home.

DOCUMENTATION IS EVERYTHING

The first thing you need to understand about documentation is that it starts with business purpose. You can't just decide to rent your house to your business and then figure out why later. You establish the business purpose first, then build an agenda that supports that purpose. This is where most people get the sequence wrong.

FOUNDATION REQUIREMENTS:

- Clear business purpose for the rental
- Detailed agenda that supports that purpose
- Signed rental agreement between you and your business
- Fair market value analysis
- Proof of payment from business to you

But what protects you when the IRS comes asking questions years later is a Comprehensive Documentation System.

To build that system, start with your agenda, but understand that an agenda alone won't be enough. Anyone can create an agenda after things have already happened. What you need is detailed meeting notes with ten to fifteen pages showing the work accomplished.

This is where AI has become invaluable. You can dictate or transcribe your entire day's work, feed it into AI, and generate thorough documentation that shows the depth of strategic work you're doing.

Document where in your house you're working throughout the day. For example:

- Home office for financial planning (9 a.m. to noon)
- Patio for strategic brainstorming (1 p.m. to 3 p.m.)
- Dining room for spreading out documents (3 p.m. to 5 p.m.)

Why does this matter? Some accountants may challenge your fair market value based on house usage. For example, if you claimed $5,000 per day but only used 30 percent of your house, they could argue for $1,500 instead. By documenting your movement throughout the property, you can help support your case for renting the entire home.

THE "AUGUSTA RULE IN A BOX" SYSTEM

Trying to apply the Augusta Rule can be complex. So, we've developed what we call the "Augusta Rule in a box," a comprehensive framework to help our clients properly implement the Augusta Rule strategy. It includes:

- Business purpose statement templates
- Rental agreement templates
- Fair market value analysis tools
- Agenda formats tailored to different planning objectives
- Documentation checklists
- Payment tracking systems

When applying this approach with clients, we use the full framework to ensure every step is well-documented. If questions ever arise about a specific day, you should be able to show exactly what was discussed, where it took place, and how it contributed to your business strategy. That level of detail can be what separates a defendable deduction from a rejected claim. In my experience, the more substantiation you have, the stronger your position tends to be.

For more information on this, you can visit:

www.AugustaRuleinaBox.com

REAL IMPLEMENTATION, REAL RESULTS

As you might imagine, many people approach the Augusta Rule solely for the tax benefit. They submit their agendas, document their days, and take deductions. Cool. They may save anywhere from $15,000 to $20,000 in taxes, depending on their situation. They're checking boxes, following the process, getting their tax benefit. And that's fine.

But some business owners see it differently. Especially the professionals with high hourly rates, like doctors, attorneys, and consultants. When you're in professional services, taking eight hours away from billable work can feel expensive. But when that eight hours of strategic planning helps you restructure your practice, delegate better, and double your capacity, the ROI becomes obvious. You understand that taking a day you can't bill to work on strategy actually multiplies your earning potential. The tax savings become secondary to the business transformation.

The difference isn't intelligence or business acumen. It's whether business owners see the Augusta Rule as just a tax strategy or as a gateway to something bigger. The tax savings can be substantial. But with strategic planning, the business transformation may far exceed the tax benefits.

WRAPPING UP

As we reach the end of Part One, we've established a foundation that could help any entrepreneurial journey. The Simplify Day Framework can help you create a monthly commitment to the future of your business. This simple discipline can create the space you need to build something that actually grows, besides giving you the possibility to unlock tangible financial benefits by applying the Augusta Rule.

With this foundation in place, we're ready to move on to the next stage where the focus shifts from simply creating space to learning how to use that space to expand and build real freedom.

PART TWO

OPTIMIZE FOR SUCCESS

IF YOU'VE MADE IT this far, the Simplify Day framework and the Augusta Rule are likely helpful for you. These strategies work at every stage of the entrepreneurial journey, and if you're still growing revenue, building your client base, and handling every part of the business yourself, they may be exactly what you need right now.

But as you move into the next phase of your financial life, especially once your income crosses the $500,000 mark, and you're on your way to making $1 million, $2 million, or more annually, you reach a point where it becomes important, even if you've been handling everything on your own, to ask, "What's the cost of not having good advisors? What's the cost of not having an integrated team? And, ultimately, what's the cost of keeping *yourself* in the quarterback seat?"

I would say there are two different costs:

1. **The cost of missing opportunities:** There may be things you're not even aware of. And oftentimes, if your team isn't proactive enough, they may not be bringing you ideas. You might be gathering that information from friends, from colleagues who are also business owners, from social media . . . whatever it might be, but there may not be a dedicated person who's actively trying to find these opportunities. And as your business evolves, opportunities that didn't make sense before may now be exactly what you need.

2. **The cost of mistakes:** The reality is, when you start getting above a $1 million of income, especially in a high-tax state like California for example, you're in the 50 percent tax bracket. When you don't take advantage of all the tax deductions that you can, that can add up. For many business owners, the assumption is that your bookkeeper got your data to your CPA, and you assume that the tax return was prepared correctly and you received all of your tax deductions. But in real life, it's actually quite common to find tax returns with mistakes, and these mistakes need to be remedied.

This combination of wanting to avoid mistakes and making sure you're aware of all the opportunities out there is a good reason to have an integrated professional team in place. Additionally, your team at $250,000 of personal income may look different than your team above $1 million. As your team grows and you're above $1 million, you've likely added a lot more complexity. That's where the financial quarterback becomes essential, and that's what we'll explore in this section of the book.

CHAPTER 4:

THE FINANCIAL QUARTERBACK: WHY IT MATTERS

MOST BUSINESS OWNERS DON'T realize they've been put in a role they were never trained for. You're coordinating professionals across multiple areas, including legal, tax, insurance, and benefits, and you're supposed to make sure they're all working together effectively. The problem is, you don't know what most of them should be doing.

When I played quarterback in high school, the hardest part wasn't throwing the ball. It was knowing what everyone else on the field was supposed to do. I had to know the routes the receivers were going to run, what the running back's job was, and what the offensive line's blocking scheme would be. I had to understand the entire play, not just my piece of it.

What made it work was that I didn't do their jobs for them. I was leading the team, making sure everyone executed their assignments at the right time.

That's exactly what a Financial Quarterback is trained to do for your professional team. A Financial Quarterback is the central professional who oversees your entire financial life and ensures that every decision, including tax, investment, legal, business, and personal is aligned and working together. Instead of managing separate professionals who operate in their own lanes, a Financial Quarterback coordinates the full team, identifies opportunities you might otherwise miss, and helps you make informed decisions with confidence. Their role is to simplify complexity, reduce the mental load, and provide proactive guidance, so you can stay focused on what matters most.

Part of getting your CERTIFIED FINANCIAL PLANNER (CFP®) certification is being well-versed in estate planning, tax planning, insurance planning, cash flow management, and benefits administration. If you're deficient in any of them, you won't pass the test. The training forces you to understand the entire playbook.

So we know what everyone's jobs should look like. We understand what the attorney should be doing with your estate plan, what the CPA should be reviewing at year-end, and what the insurance professional should be evaluating as your business grows. We're not doing the legal work; we're not doing the tax compliance; we're not writing the insurance policies. But we can lead the team and make sure everyone is executing in sync.

The problem is that, as a business owner, you get thrust into the quarterback role without any of that training. You're supposed to coordinate professionals you don't fully understand, making decisions about strategies you've never been taught. Imagine being a coach trying to run a football team with no quarterback on the field. Who's calling the plays? Who's reading the defense and adjusting at the line? Who's making sure the offensive line knows their blocking assignments while the receivers are running their routes?

That's the chaos many business owners can find themselves in. And it may feel even harder because you didn't sign up for this job. You became an entrepreneur to build a business, to serve customers, or to create something. Managing a team of business professionals wasn't part of the plan. But success created complexity, and complexity created the need for specialists, and suddenly, you're spending hours every month just trying to keep everyone on the same page.

In this chapter, we'll look at what it costs to coordinate professionals, why the Virtual Family Office model provides better protection, and how to tell the difference between professionals who are truly serving you versus those who are just going through the motions.

THE COST OF BEING THE QUARTERBACK

As your business grows and your income increases, the challenges you face start to change. As we extensively discussed in Part One, when you're just getting started, being the quarterback of your business professionals might work. But once you break through higher income levels, say $500,000 or more, that role starts to wear you out.

By this stage, most business owners already have a team in place, CPA, bookkeeper, attorney, insurance agent, payroll provider and more. But nobody's making sure they work together. So, you end up acting as the quarterback for your professional team. And I know you're probably making things work, but being the point person for every decision, every tax question, and every operational detail can feel exhausting.

This is where smart use of your resources comes in. In the last couple chapters, we walked through strategies like the Simplify Day and the Augusta Rule. If you implemented the Augusta Rule appropriately, you may be saving somewhere between $6,000 and $24,000 a year. But don't pocket those savings.

I know that might sound counterintuitive. You might be thinking "You've just shown me how to save money and now you're telling me not to keep it?" But what I want you to understand is that those savings may be enough to hire a professional who can quarterback your team. You've just freed up money that could help you reduce stress, reclaim your time, and focus on what really matters, like growing your business, enjoying your life, and spending time with your family.

To illustrate what this can look like, consider a hypothetical business owner who runs a successful practice with a steady stream of clients and a strong reputation. On the outside, everything may appear to be running smoothly. But behind the scenes, they feel overwhelmed.

They have a full professional team, but none of it is truly coordinated. Everyone is working in their own lane, and every time something goes wrong, the issue lands right back on the owner's desk.

What this business owner really wants is simple. They want to go to work, take care of their clients, and get home at a reasonable hour to spend time with their family without having to spend evenings dealing with payroll problems and tax questions.

And that's exactly the pain point so many business owners face. They didn't start their business to become an operations manager, an HR coordinator, or a financial controller. They just wanted to do the work they love and build a meaningful life around it.

This is where a financial quarterback can step in, not to take control away, but to take ownership of coordination. The quarterback can help ensure the team is aligned, the plan is clear, and decisions aren't happening reactively under pressure. The goal is to keep everyone accountable and moving in the same direction, rather than pushing the burden back on the owner.

In a scenario like this, the first year of building that coordination typically takes work. There may be a lot of pieces to connect. But once the foundation is established and the roles are clear, the ongoing effort tends to become lighter.

Over time, when something comes up, whether it's a payroll issue, a quarterly tax payment, a tax planning question, or a 401(k)-related decision, the business owner doesn't have to get dragged into the weeds. They can go to the quarterback, who assembles the right people and leads the solution. The owner remains informed and involved, but not burdened. They can focus on their practice and their family.

The real value shows up not just in saving money or improving operations but in giving the business owner back the time and peace of mind they were looking for.

This kind of experience isn't unusual. In fact, this is the point where many business owners start to realize that having a team isn't the same as having a coordinated team.

So, a question usually comes up:

"What exactly does it look like when someone steps into that quarterback role?"

That's usually where the idea of the Virtual Family Office comes in.

VIRTUAL FAMILY OFFICE VS ONE-STOP-SHOP

We've already discussed that being someone's financial quarterback is really taking the lead role in coordinating their entire team. But there's a fancy term used to describe that same idea. Virtual Family Office (VFO).

Traditionally, as families move north of $20 million in net worth, they tend to establish a Family Office, which is a structure where all their professionals, from tax to legal to investments, sit under one roof. But a true family office isn't typically accessible unless you're well over $100 million. That's a huge barrier, and it leaves a gap for families who would benefit from that level of coordination but don't have enough to build an in-house team.

That's where the VFO comes in. It works like a family office, but instead of everything being housed internally, the professionals stay independent. We step into the quarterback role, coordinating the team, so the client gets the same cohesive experience without needing a nine-figure net worth. That means not everyone is under the same roof, but we work together to create a cohesive team for our clients.

In my opinion, that's a better structure because it provides a lot more checks and balances, and it brings different perspectives to the table. We don't have a monopoly on all the best ideas. A lot of the strategies we bring to clients, we learned from other professionals solving problems for different clients. That cross-pollination only works when you have independent professionals collaborating.

When everything is bundled together, you can run into some real risks. If you're unhappy with one service, you often end up having to replace the entire team, which is really disruptive. And with too much authority sitting in one place with no oversight, the risk of conflict (or even fraud) could go up.

You've probably heard some horror stories in the news with entertainers or athletes who had one business manager handling everything, and it turned out that person was stealing from them or making terrible decisions.

Our approach is different. Fidelity custodies our clients' assets. We don't have custody. We don't pay bills for clients. You don't want all that power under one roof, in our humble opinion.

The flexibility advantage matters, too. If you're unhappy with one professional on your team, you can pull them out and insert someone new. The rest of the team stays together. We don't have one dedicated CPA we work with. We have multiple, based on the client's size, needs, stage of life, and sometimes even geographic location.

For estate planning attorneys, we probably have a list of over twenty. Then it's a matter of filtering. Where are they located? How complex is the estate? If it's a $30 million estate or more, they might need a specific attorney. If they just need a basic trust, that's a different referral.

The more specialized the professionals are, the better. We love it when someone says, "I only work with businesses doing $10 million in revenue and up." That's a very clear niche, and it makes pairing them with the right clients so much easier. When somebody says, "Oh, I do everything for everyone," that's actually harder to work with.

By leading a team of independent experts, we give families the benefits of a family office at much more accessible wealth levels, often starting around $5 million, without the downsides of a fully centralized model. It creates the feel and function of a family office but with more flexibility and long-term stability.

HOW COLLABORATION WORKS

Getting professionals to collaborate effectively starts with eliminating unnecessary friction. Take bookkeepers, for example. The old-school approach means the bookkeeper has the data, and anytime you need something, you have to request it. For example, you ask for a profit and loss statement, and they send it. Then you need to dig deeper into a specific line item, so they send another report. You ask for a change, and another report follows.

Or even worse, you ask the client for information, they go to their bookkeeper, the bookkeeper sends it to the client, and the client sends it back to you. Then you realize that report isn't comprehensive enough, and you need something else. It turns into an endless game of telephone that wastes everyone's time and costs the client money.

Our approach is simple. Whenever possible, we ask for read-only access to QuickBooks Online. That way, we can review the information directly, identify what we need, and provide timely updates. It streamlines communication, reduces back-and-forth, and ultimately saves the client both time and money without adding extra steps for anyone.

When it comes to accountants, we schedule year-end planning meetings to combine their "rearview mirror" perspective with our forward-looking strategy. With estate planning attorneys, I prefer to be in the room with clients, since we understand the family dynamics and their long-term goals. That puts us in a position to advocate for them. A lot of times, clients don't fully understand the landscape of what the professional is going to do, so they don't know what questions to ask or how to approach the conversation. Our expertise fills that gap. We can be their voice, with them present, as they're making potentially major decisions for their family. It's not just about avoiding miscommunication. It's about being a trusted partner by their side when these conversations happen. With insurance professionals, we serve as a second set of eyes on their recommendations.

At the core of all this, our role is to advocate for the client and ensure execution.

THE THREE KEYS TO A STRONG TEAM

Building an integrated professional team comes down to three things:

1. WILLINGNESS TO COLLABORATE

You want professionals with low egos who understand that at the end of the day, we all serve the client. The professionals who protect their territory and refuse to work with others create friction that hurts the clients' interests.

2. RIGHT SKILL SET FOR YOUR CURRENT STAGE

Our default is always to keep your current professionals. We're not coming in to blow everything up.

But we do need to assess and make sure they can do the job you need today. Sometimes we find that good professionals have more capabilities than the client is using. They've fallen into a rut because the client only ever asked for a narrow set of services. A little push might get more value out of the relationship without replacing anyone.

Other times, you've genuinely outgrown someone. The person who was perfect when you were doing $500,000 in revenue might not have the expertise you need at $5 million. That's not anyone's fault. It's just the reality of growth.

And then there are the C players . . . the ones who drain your energy, drag you down from a time perspective, and might even cost you money through bad advice or gaps in coverage. Those need to be addressed.

3. COMMUNICATION PLAN

Without direct lines of communication between professionals, you may end up playing the telephone game. Time and money can get eaten up when the client sits in the center of every conversation.

With a proper communication plan, the work happens behind the scenes. The client can watch it all and can interject if they want to, but they don't have to manage it. That's the whole point of having a professional team in the first place.

GETTING OUT OF THE MIDDLE

When you reach a certain level of complexity in your business and your wealth, it might be worth taking a fresh assessment. Who on your team is delivering massive value? Who's quarterbacking all these relationships? If it's you, maybe it's time to consider a change.

At the end of the day, having a good quarterback should simplify things for everyone. You have a leader taking charge, requiring some level of efficiency because there's now a cohesive strategy in place. That efficiency saves money, but it also saves you time. And for many people, time is their most precious resource.

When we do our job effectively, it's great to see we're saving money. But if we can save time, save the headaches and stress, and focus on optimizing the results, that's where the real value shows up. It creates leverage. You get more from what you're doing without managing every piece of it yourself.

For most of our clients, and this includes me as a business owner, I want to be efficient with my time when I manage the business aspects, especially the financial ones. That way I can spend more time on things I enjoy, like mentoring and building my company and spending time with my wife and my kids. Doing this effectively frees you up to spend time where you want to spend it, instead of letting this drag you down.

When things aren't coordinated, you're usually getting brought in to make a decision under pressure, and there's a level of urgency because you're getting pulled in around a deadline. It's really hard to pivot from whatever life looks like for you to problem-solve on something urgent.

Of course, there'll always be some uncertainty in life. But having a strategy or a plan can take a lot of that uncertainty out. And when we do face uncertainty or something changes, we can adapt a lot faster because the plan is already in place. We've created a framework for how we're going to make decisions. The goal is that you stop managing your team and get back to leading your business.

That's where your time should be spent, anyway.

CHAPTER 5:

PLANNING YOUR IDEAL YEAR - PLANNING IN ORDER TO BE SUCCESSFUL

ONCE YOU HAVE THE right team in place and you're not stuck in the middle acting as a quarterback, you finally have time to lead your business. But how can you make sure you're going to use this time well?

Having a clear vision of where you want to be is what ultimately allows you to be more successful. It's really hard to make good decisions in the present when you don't know where you're going. Things tend to feel easier when you have a picture of where you want to be in the future. Once you know where you're heading, you can work backward and ask, "Are the decisions I'm making today moving me toward that long-term success?"

Benjamin Franklin once said, "If you fail to plan, you're planning to fail," and that's true. That's the reminder I want to share with you here. Even with a financial quarterback in place, you still have to set the vision for your family and for your company.

Part of our job as quarterbacks is to design the playbook, a guide to support that work, a roadmap to help you understand what you're going after and then actually do it. But we can't replace you.

That's also why the Simplify Day exists. It frees you up, so you have the space to plan, to think, to make the decisions that move your business forward. And because you have that dedicated day each month to handle all that work, you can be fully present with your team and clients on your "non-Simplify Days."

That was something I recognized when I was scaling my firm.

Early on, as we were adding new clients to the firm, it was becoming increasingly difficult to remember everyone's data, like their name, date of birth, spouse, children, business structure, and all the complexity that goes into understanding an individual and their financial life.

So we created what we call a CFO, which stands for Client Financial Organizer. In our world, it's essentially like a doctor's chart. It's a four to ten page document that contains everything you need to know about a client. If I or anyone on the team spend just a few minutes reading it, we can confidently run any meeting and provide sound advice.

That's because the CFO holds the core elements of financial planning along with key family details, company information, and personal preferences. It's the foundation that allows us to truly know our clients.

But getting to that point wasn't easy. Developing these organizers took an incredible amount of time. Not just creating the main template but developing it upfront and customizing it for every client.

One of my mentors told me something that really stuck with me during this process. At the time, I was frustrated. I was spending hours getting deep into the details, trying to develop the perfect solution. So I asked him probably a simple and naive question. "Is this really a good use of my time?"

His answer was clear and direct. He said, "Doing it this way the first time probably is a good use of your time. But the second time, it should be a little faster. And the third time, faster still."

What he was really telling me was that the goal isn't just to do the work; it's to build the process. Each repetition should make you more efficient, more confident, and more precise. That advice completely reframed how I approached problem-solving. It reminded me that the long hours spent refining something the first time aren't wasted. They're an investment in building systems that make everything easier down the road.

Today, the CFO has become the foundation of our business. I can't imagine walking into a client meeting without that level of understanding of who they are. It's proven to be one of the best investments we've made because, at the end of the day, our business is really about people.

This chapter is about how that same principle applies to planning your ideal year. We'll look at how monthly Simplify

Days connect to your long-term vision, why most entrepreneurial goals fail without systematic check-ins, how to balance the constant pull between self, family, and business, and why recalibration matters more than perfection.

CONNECTING MONTHLY RHYTHM TO LONG-TERM VISION

Every month, the Simplify Day gives me a chance to reconnect to my goals. When you start with a ten year target and work backward through a three year picture, one year goals, and quarterly rocks, it creates focus on what really matters. Simplify Day gives me the rhythm to make sure the long-term vision doesn't drift into the background.

This framework was inspired by the book *Traction* by Gino Wickman[3]. It's part of what's called the Entrepreneurial Operating System, or EOS. I adopted it in 2017 when I was about fifteen years into my entrepreneurial journey. And, honestly, it transformed how I ran the business.

Before that, I felt like I was trying to fly a plane while still building it. I've always loved innovation and moving the firm forward with new ideas. But I was also constantly distracted. So, the line to our success was pretty choppy because it was driven by my constant need to innovate without enough structure.

When I read Traction, it simplified all the noise I had in my head around what it took to build a business. It created a framework that made everything way less noisy for me.

3 Wickman, G. (2012). Traction. BenBella Books, Inc.

I've always had a sense of where I wanted to go. I spend a lot of time thinking about the future because having goals that stretch you . . . maybe even feel too high . . . creates something to strive for. By going out on a ten year timeline, you give yourself some grace because it's far enough out that you can be really optimistic, even overly ambitious. The ten year gives me this aspirational place I'd love to reach. But the reality is that life happens. There's no straight path to that.

As an example, when I was twenty-eight, I set a goal to go from zero revenue to $1 million in ten years. That seemed realistic and something that would provide for my family. I hit that goal in five years, from 2003 to 2007, right before the financial crisis.

So I reset the ten-year target to go from $1 million to $2.5 million. Then the financial crisis hit. We retraced from $1 million back to about $700,000. It took a full ten year period from 2009 to 2018 to get to $2 million.

That sideways movement wasn't wasted time; it was foundational. When you're growing from zero to $1 million, you're just running with your head cut off. But when the financial crisis hit, that period became about building the foundation. I started asking myself:

- What does this organization need to look like?
- What processes need to be in place?
- Who are the right people to have on the team?

Out of necessity, we had to become structurally strong. My focus shifted from chasing expansion to building a healthy company, one that could truly serve our clients for the long term, not just grow for growth's sake.

Then over the last five years, we've gone from $2 million to over $6 million. Growth became a lot easier because we put the hard work in to build the foundation.

For most people, if you're setting a ten year target, you're probably going to revisit it every three to five years. You first need to assess if you are on track. And if you're ahead, it's time to set a new objective that's even bigger.

The three year picture is way more relevant because it's within reach. Three years goes by pretty quickly. Many people set really short-term goals because they're not even envisioning a bigger and better future. That's why I like to go out for ten years. It feels aspirational. But then it allows you to focus on the near-term goals where you're asking, "If I want to get there, what things have to be true here in the near term?"

WHY SOME GOALS TEND FAIL: THE FOCUS PROBLEM

During my Simplify Days, I tend to stay focused on the areas where I add the most value, both in business and in my personal life. I lean on this concept from a Strategic Coach called Unique Ability. For me, that comes down to two things. I'm a multiplier, meaning I can see challenges and find new solutions to move things forward. And I'm also a leader in the sense that I can attract the right people and get them excited about a bigger vision.

The challenge I used to face was setting a lot of annual goals with no real mechanism to check in. A year would pass and I'd look back with regret. Why didn't I get this done? The truth was, it just wasn't top of mind. Simplify Days solve that problem. They give me focus time each month to stay anchored in my unique ability and make progress on the right things.

Let me give you a concrete example. Say you set two major goals at the beginning of the year:

- I want to exercise three days a week for cardio and two days a week for strength training.
- I want to read twenty books this year.

Those are good goals. You set them as objectives, and in the back of your head, you know they're prioritized.

But unless you have a regular way of checking in, six months go by, and you were to have completed seventy-five cardio workouts over twenty-five weeks. That's three workouts per week. You've only had fifty. You're twenty-five workouts behind halfway through the year. How are you going to catch up?

You wanted to read twenty books. You've only read two. Now you have eighteen books to get done in six months.

When you're that far behind at the midpoint, it can feel impossible. You start to beat yourself up. The goals feel out of reach. And often, you just give up entirely.

But with monthly check-ins, if you're behind after one month, it's very easy to course correct. You can reset and say, "Okay, I need to do four days of cardio this month to catch up," or "I need to read three books this month instead of the one and a half I originally planned." When you're evaluating more regularly, you're a better accountability partner for yourself.

We're going to go through stages of life where we have fatigue, life events, we're busier, traveling, business is crazy. Life will happen. Those thirty day check-ins on the Simplify Days can allow you to course correct on a regular basis.

Unless you have things top of mind, you're less likely to be measuring. And generally, unless you're just insanely disciplined (which I would not say is a characteristic of a lot of us entrepreneurs), you may fall short. Then you look back at the year and realize you didn't accomplish half of what you set out to do. But if you do a check-in every single month, the probability of success goes way up.

The one year objectives become a key reference point when I'm doing my Simplify Days. I make sure that the activities I'm doing today are all working together and moving in the same direction. It also provides a good framework where, as an entrepreneur, I can get distracted. But then it forces me to look at how this fits into the one year objective.

I'm usually spending two to three hours either listening to podcasts or reading every day, so I get so many fresh ideas. It can be exhausting for my team to have to absorb them. So, creating a one year plan of the top two or three things we're going to focus on gives me a filter. If I have some new idea and it doesn't fit under those goals, I just put it in a parking lot unless it's something that's an emergency, and I have to make a change.

But if it's just a really good idea that doesn't fit within my one year framework, I've done a much better job of creating discipline to put it aside for a future time. When I get to year-end and I'm setting new goals, I look at that list of ideas I didn't implement.

A lot of times, I look at it and think, *"Okay, that doesn't make sense anymore."* Sometimes giving an idea a little time and distance is all it takes to realize it wasn't a good one.

But it also gives you the framework to help set your next one year goals because now you have a parking lot of ideas. You can identify what makes sense, unpack that a little bit more, and see if that's something you want to set as a goal for the next year.

The Simplify Days force discipline around making sure you're doing the right things because your goals should work within some framework of what the longer-term goals look like.

BALANCING PERSONAL WELL-BEING, FAMILY, AND BUSINESS

Entrepreneurs are constantly pulled between business, family, and personal well-being. If you're not healthy as an individual, if you're not taking care of yourself and prioritizing what matters personally, it can be harder to show up as your best version. That may directly impact your business.

In my experience, it's clear that optimizing every aspect of your life at once is incredibly difficult and maybe even impossible. I haven't met anyone who can be 100 percent disciplined with their health and wellness, 100 percent fully present with their spouse and kids, and 100 percent engaged with everything their business needs. That level of engagement would be a superpower, and although I'd love to do it, I haven't found that ability yet.

Life naturally shifts, and priorities change. Sometimes, something breaks and requires your attention. That could be a business with cash flow issues, a strained relationship with one of your kids, or communication breaking down with your spouse. Maybe you're facing some health issues and suddenly that becomes urgent. Sometimes you choose to shift your focus, and sometimes the situation forces your hand. You can't prepare for everything.

The truth is that whenever you push one area up to 100 percent, it almost always means the other areas drop. For example, if I get hyper-focused on my workouts and personal wellness and get that area to 100 percent, then business might slide down a little bit. The attention has to shift somewhere. And because everything is connected, that balance is always in motion.

A constant balancing act is not meant to be a negative thing. It's important for you to stay focused because business, family, and personal well-being matter.

For me, I know I'm not going to be perfect because it's literally impossible, but I want the ability to honestly assess how I'm doing. When I know some area needs attention, I need to dial it up and be more purposeful there. That's what a Simplify Day does. It helps you to do check-ins to assess these areas:

- How are you taking care of yourself?
- How's your energy, and how are you leading your business?
- What's happening with your family?
- Are you leading your family in the proper manner?
- Are your relationships healthy?

To be honest, during the first five years of my business, I did not have the kind of balance that I would have liked. When I went through a divorce about five years into starting the business, I definitely neglected the family side of things, which was painful. It was a really hard time.

When you're in survival mode and your business isn't successful, you can't provide for your family, and that can have an emotional toll on you. Your focus areas probably aren't fully aligned with that perfect view of yourself. But out of necessity, it creates that dynamic.

The insecure time of running a business tends to be hard on humans. It can be hard on families because it's difficult to be the best version of yourself when you're still trying to make things happen.

I've always done a good job (well, after those first five years) of creating some balance. Most entrepreneurs have to decide what phase they're in their journey. When you're financially secure, it's a lot easier to maintain that balance.

Now, I've been with Carmen for fifteen years, and we recently got married in 2024. She got the better version of me because I got through that really difficult time around the survival part of the business.

The Simplify Day and this entire offering grew out of my own experiences. I built these solutions to address the specific pain points I faced personally, as well as the challenges I've helped other entrepreneurs navigate over the years.

What I've learned is that, sometimes, you just need to take a pause and ask:

1. Am I living with intention, or am I letting life happen to me?

2. What needs my attention most right now, in my health, my family, and my business?
3. What commitments have I made, and am I honoring them with my actions?

It allows you to refocus. That's why this is so critical to me. I know that if I had some of these tools early on, if I was equipped with this better mindset and thinking, it would have made me a much more effective person. This is especially true when looking at balancing my own health, my time with family, and attention to the business.

MONTHLY PLANNING FOR YOUR BUSINESS

A big part of where the Simplify Days come in is they create structure for the business owner. When you're not on a Simplify Day, which is the majority of your time, you're working in the business, serving your end customer, working with your patients, or mentoring your employees.

For most of us, because we're technically proficient in the field we're in, those are the things we love doing. That's where we want to spend our time. But all of the noise around running the business starts to seep into our day-to-day. It distracts us. It sucks energy because these are things we don't want to do, but they're required. As an entrepreneur, you're the one running the ship. You're making sure things are moving forward.

This is where the Simplify Day truly makes an impact. While we may not be the ones driving sales, we enable people to show up as their most effective selves for their team and clients. This is possible because they've used that dedicated day to eliminate the noise and address key business challenges.

When you have that dedicated day, you have a placeholder for that work. When you think, "I've got to work on this project" or "I need to make sure we improve our financial numbers," you know exactly where it goes. And then on the days where you're not doing the Simplify Day, you're fully present. You're not distracted by all the administrative burdens and the things pulling at you.

It's hard to multiply things when there's chaos. Even as you grow and have more success, it's important to consider if this is accidental or repeatable. That's where we try to get our entrepreneurs thinking. Because if they're repeatable, then you can staff and build processes around it.

THE COMPOUND EFFECT OF CONSISTENCY

You need consistency, not perfection. Keep showing up month after month. After a year, you may start to see real changes. After several years, the compound effect can be significant.

You probably won't be great at this right away. Some Simplify Days will be amazing. Others will be just okay. That's normal. Give yourself some grace.

The pause to reflect and refocus is critical. You become a monthly accountability partner for yourself. The important work you keep putting off is not going away. But with monthly Simplify Days connected to your long-term vision, you can create a place to get it done. And more importantly, you can have the structure to keep showing up as the best version of yourself for your business, your family, and yourself.

RESOURCES

Reading suggestions:

Traction. Wickman, G. (2012). BenBella Books, Inc.

The E-myth revisited: why most small businesses don't work and what to do about it. Gerber, M. E. (2017). HarperBusiness.

CHAPTER 6:

THE LIFETIME TAX PHILOSOPHY - BEYOND THIS YEAR'S BILL

IN THE LAST CHAPTER, we talked about thinking in longer timeframes by setting ten year targets, building three year pictures, and breaking those down into annual goals with monthly check-ins. That extended view is what allows you to be ambitious without getting overwhelmed.

That same logic of looking further out also applies to your taxes, which are one of the single largest expenses you'll deal with as an entrepreneur.

In terms of taxes, I believe that we're offering a kind of leadership that runs almost counter to the instincts of many business owners and even some CPAs. People tend to be wired to save money today. It's natural, maybe even evolutionary, to want to protect whatever is right in front of you. So our approach can feel counterintuitive. Instead of focusing only on preserving cash this year, we look at the long-term plan of someone's life and business.

For example, I'm in my early fifties, so when I think about my tax philosophy, I'm thinking about what will unfold over the next several decades. How do I make smart decisions today? Would that mean paying more taxes today to pay less later?

The benefit of this approach is the compounding effect of those good decisions. In the short term, you'll probably feel some pain. But because of how money compounds over time, the long-term savings really add up and become significant down the road. When you're so focused on just this year, you may be missing the big picture.

Imagine a business owner who's having a down income year, dropping from $700,000 to $300,000. At $300,000, they still have room to generate about $50,000 more income while staying in the relatively low 24 percent tax bracket. In most cases, we'd recommend a Roth conversion. Take that $50,000, recognize the income now, and pay the 24 percent tax. Since their income fell from the top 37 percent bracket down to 24 percent, it can make sense to add some taxable income.

Now, let's say this business owner is fifty years old and won't touch this money until age seventy-five. The $50,000 they paid tax on today could double three times over twenty-five years with typical market returns. The $50,000 could become $100,000, then $200,000, then $400,000. At that point, they'd have an account worth $400,000 and owe zero taxes on withdrawal. They paid tax on $50,000 at a lower bracket than they'd typically be in. That's the compounding benefit of this mindset.

If you've built a successful business that generates over $1 million annually, you're essentially a permanently high earner who will likely face a high tax bracket for the long haul.

Because of that, when you experience a down year or find yourself with excessive write-offs, you should recognize that moment as a strategic opportunity to optimize your lifetime tax bill.

Besides, life isn't a straight line for business owners. Some years you may be in a very high bracket and want to accelerate deductions; other years income could be artificially low, perhaps because of a large purchase and bonus depreciation.

Imagine someone who made a significant asset purchase a few years ago. By using bonus depreciation, they were able to substantially reduce their taxable income for that year.

That kind of temporary drop in income is exactly the type of planning window we pay close attention to.

Now, in that same scenario, we can model what it might look like if partial Roth conversions were done during that lower-income year. By shifting income into a more favorable tax bracket at that moment, you can potentially create long-term tax efficiency over the course of retirement.

When you see it mapped out over a lifetime, it often becomes much clearer how impactful those decisions can be.

Being mindful of what the future may hold and making thoughtful decisions with the information available today is a great tax philosophy.

These examples connect directly to what we'll explore in this chapter. We'll discuss how to think about taxes differently; not just what you pay this year, but what you may pay over your entire lifetime.

We'll examine why some commonly used strategies may not always lead to the most efficient long-term outcomes, and how building a structured approach to Tax Due Diligence™

can potentially improve outcomes and create meaningful tax savings over time.

THE CORE PHILOSOPHY: LIFETIME VS. SINGLE YEAR

Most people think success with taxes means one of two things . . . they paid less this year, or they got a refund. But the truth is if you're getting a refund, that means you overpaid all year. You essentially gave the government an interest-free loan when you could've had that money working for you. That's not a win. That's just poor cash-flow management.

Our philosophy is different. We believe that it's really important to focus on your lifetime tax bill, not just what you owe in any single year. Sometimes that means paying more in taxes today, so you pay less over your lifetime.

Imagine someone in their late sixties, planning to retire within the next few years, who is considering contributing $85,000 to a retirement account based on recommendations from their accountant and bookkeeper. On the surface, it may seem like a reasonable decision.

However, when you take a closer look, a potential mismatch can appear.

At that stage, the contribution might generate tax savings at a lower marginal rate, say, around 17.5 percent. But if those funds are withdrawn in the near future during retirement, they could be taxed at a higher rate, such as 24 percent, depending on the individual's overall income picture.

In that scenario, what initially looked like a tax-saving strategy may not result in the most efficient outcome over time.

The problem is that many people focus on one question. "How do I reduce my tax bill this year?" But nobody is asking, "What does this cost me later?" When you're working with a wealth advisor for potentially the next thirty or forty years, our goal isn't to drive your tax bill to zero every single year. In fact, paying more in taxes over time usually means your income is growing, and your business is doing well.

What we really focus on is the big picture. If we can estimate how much tax you'll pay over your lifetime, our job is to help you keep that total number as low as possible through smart, long-term planning. But we can't plan in a vacuum; we have to look at the economic reality heading our way.

For instance, our federal government owes nearly $40 trillion. To pay that off, the government may need to increase taxes in the future. If that happens, people who haven't planned with a lifetime tax strategy in mind could end up paying more taxes down the road.

There's a specific window where this becomes critical, between ages fifty-five and seventy.

Before age sixty-seven or seventy, you haven't started collecting Social Security yet. Before seventy-two, seventy-three, or seventy-five (it used to be 70 1/2, but they keep pushing it back), you haven't hit Required Minimum Distributions from your retirement accounts. This window is your unique opportunity to set yourself up for embracing the lifetime tax philosophy.

During this time, we can map out your future income streams, including investments, dividends, and rental income and forecast your lifetime tax liability. Then we can make strategic decisions about when to recognize income and when to take deductions.

Business owners, in particular, miss these opportunities. When they have a bad year, they're relieved to pay less tax. But we see it differently. A bad year can be an opportunity for Roth conversions and other strategies that recognize income at lower rates. Don't let a bad year go to waste.

THE YEAR-END CAR PURCHASE TRAP

Now, something that drives me crazy is the year-end car purchase, which is a very common tax strategy.

Every December, many business owners rush to buy vehicles over 6,000 pounds to get the Section 179 deduction. Take that $100,000 Escalade, and you might save up to $24,000 in taxes this year by writing it off completely.

But if you're in the 24 percent bracket this year and heading toward 32 percent or 37 percent in future years, you could save more by spreading out the deductions and taking them when they're worth more.

This isn't rocket science; it's just math. But emotions drive these decisions more than logic. Nobody wants to write a check to the IRS today, even if it saves them more by delaying the deduction. CPAs know this, which is why they often optimize for the current year rather than having the harder conversation about long-term strategy.

Our approach requires discipline and a longer view. We model out scenarios, show the numbers, and explain the time value of money. Some clients get it immediately. Others nod along until I mention they need to write a check this year, then suddenly the long-term benefits don't seem as compelling.

Real tax planning isn't about avoiding taxes but paying them strategically. If your main tax strategy involves buying something you don't need at year-end, you're not planning. You're just reacting. And over a lifetime, that difference can cost you hundreds of thousands of dollars.

THE TAX DUE DILIGENCE SYSTEM

Alongside our tax philosophy, we've built our Tax Due Diligence™ process. This is our annual process where we review tax returns to make sure the strategies were implemented correctly.

It's not a formal audit; it's a confirmation that everything we planned was actually implemented, including Roth conversions, backdoor Roths, Augusta Rule, and various deductions . . . whatever strategies were part of the plan.

Many people send their information to their CPA once a year. Then they get a letter back, saying, "You owe this much," or "You're getting a refund." A DocuSign shows up in their inbox, they sign it, and that's it. The return gets filed away, and everyone assumes it's good. But almost no one takes a second look to confirm the return is actually right.

But mistakes happen (we're all human, right?). In 2021, we reviewed more than 250 personal and business tax returns and identified issues in over 20 percent of them. This is an eye-opening reminder that even well-intentioned filings can miss key details. In one case, we even uncovered a six-figure income overstatement that could materially affect both taxes and planning decisions, reinforcing why an independent review can be a valuable extra layer of due diligence.

That experience made it clear something was missing. Everyone just assumes their taxes are right, but what if a big deduction got left out because you forgot to send one document? Or your accountant, who's juggling hundreds of returns, simply didn't catch it? That's a huge lost opportunity.

So we built a solution. Our Tax Due Diligence™ process came out of this need for an extra layer of review. It works as a second set of eyes to protect you from eventual mistakes. Clients want to make sure every deduction they're entitled to gets captured. And since many people aren't equipped to comb through their own tax returns, we created a system to do it for them.

As I mentioned, our objective is not auditing anyone's taxes. What we do is a deep dive, a proactive review guided by checklists that help us verify what's been done, what might be missing, and whether each client's tax plan actually got executed the way we intended. It's all part of this broader lifetime tax philosophy. If our goal is to minimize taxes over the long term, we also need to make sure each year's return reflects the plan.

When we started looking closely at our client's taxes, we realized most of the issues weren't because of negligence or bad accounting; they were simply missed opportunities.

Tax planning tends to be reactive instead of proactive. But by being proactive, we've uncovered many ways to improve results, from how clients pay themselves to how they take advantage of parts of the tax code like PTE and QBI deductions.

That's why we built a forty-point personal checklist and a twenty-five-point business checklist to help identify opportunities that might apply to each client. Not every strategy fits every situation, but even small adjustments can make a real difference.

A good example is the backdoor Roth IRA. A lot of our clients aren't eligible to contribute directly to a Roth, so we help them make a nondeductible IRA contribution and later convert it to a Roth, tax-advantaged, through this backdoor strategy.

When we review a client's return, we know exactly what to look for. If that line doesn't match what it should, we flag it and work with their CPA to get it fixed. And it happens often enough that catching it makes a real difference.

At the end of the day, it all comes back to being proactive. A lot of tax opportunities just go unnoticed because no one's looking for them. Our goal is to change that, to bring some clarity, some structure, and a second set of eyes to a process most people never think twice about.

THE LONG GAME

The reality CPAs face is that most of these conversations happen when deadlines are looming. Corporate returns are due in five days and individual filing deadlines are coming up fast. They just want to get the taxes done and filed. It's not that they're giving bad advice. It's just that there's no time for the longer conversations.

And honestly? Many business owners don't want that conversation either. When we start talking about lifetime tax optimization and forecasting bracket positions five years out, they just say, "As long as you know what you're doing, go run with it."

That's why we don't just talk about it. We map it out, and we walk them through why this makes sense.

That kind of illustration makes everything clearer for the clients. That's why whenever we onboard a new client, we do a free tax assessment. We have a tool we've built that highlights all these planning opportunities so they can see firsthand how our tax philosophy would apply to them.

And I call this a philosophy for a reason. Not everyone shares this perspective (and that's fine!). It requires a level of discipline that not every advisor or client is willing to commit to.

Our goal is for clients to pay less in total taxes over their entire life than they would have otherwise. That's the outcome we work toward.

RESOURCES

Reading suggestions:

Profit First: Transform Your Business From a Cash-Eating Monster to a Money-Making Machine. Michalowicz, M. (n.d.).

Simple Numbers, Straight Talk, Big Profits! 4 Keys to Unlock Your Business Potential. Crabtree, G., & Harzog, B. B. (2011). Greenleaf Book Group Press.

CHAPTER 7:

FROM OPERATOR TO ENTREPRENEUR: REDEFINING SUCCESS

BEING AN ENTREPRENEUR IS complicated. The complexity never goes away. Even with the right frameworks, strong systems, and a great team, there will always be difficult decisions and real tradeoffs. That's just part of the work. The goal isn't to eliminate complexity; it's to stop being consumed by it.

That's one of the reasons we built our Simplify brand in the first place and why we named it simplify365®. The name came from recognizing something obvious but important. Most business owners are thinking about their business or the impact of their business 365 days a year. And if that is true, how you organize that thinking matters just as much as what you do with it.

So, if we could make that experience more intentional, more organized, and less reactive, the benefits could extend beyond the financial. They might show up in leadership, in relationships, in energy, and in clarity.

Over time, I've learned that structure doesn't restrict entrepreneurs. It frees them. When structure replaces chaos, clarity tends to follow. And with clarity comes a shift that's far more meaningful than growth alone. They move from reaction to intention.

This chapter is about that shift. We're going to walk through how that evolution happens and how you move from handling everything yourself to building something that serves all the different layers.

THE BOTTLENECK I DIDN'T SEE

When you think about growing a business, a big part of that comes down to trust. Clients have to trust you, and you have to trust yourself and your team. And a lot of that trust shows up in how you manage delegation.

I've already mentioned how I love solving problems. Challenges energize me. I dig in, connect the dots, and work to find a solution. That trait served me incredibly well early on, and for a long time, I saw it as one of my greatest strengths as a leader.

What I didn't realize was that solving all the problems myself was quietly holding the business back. When you step in too quickly, you don't give your team enough space to develop. When you answer every question, you can unintentionally train people to bring you problems instead of solutions. Over time, you become the bottleneck.

The real change for me came when I finally understood the difference between delegating work and delegating coordination. By that point, I had already delegated tasks by hiring smart, capable professionals. But decisions still flowed up to me. My team was competent, yet dependent. And as the business grew, that dependency became heavier.

Things began to change when I stopped trying to be the best problem solver in the room and started asking better questions. These questions forced thinking, ownership, and accountability to move down.

That didn't happen by accident. It happened because I finally created dedicated time to step out of the day-to-day and look at the business objectively. That's when the business began to scale without me being at the center of every decision.

The Simplify Day exists to create that space. When you have a dedicated day each month to address strategy, structure, priorities, and performance, you gain a clearer vision of where to go.

Looking back, that's what marked my real transition from operator to entrepreneur.

REDEFINING SUCCESS

Early success is easy to measure. You can see it in revenue, growth, and survival. Later on, success becomes quieter and, in my experience, far more meaningful.

At that point, success might show up in how often the business needs you, whether decisions improve without your involvement, and whether progress continues even when you step back.

It also shows up in how you spend your time and whether that time is focused where you add the most value.

A truly successful business is not just one that generates more income. It is one that creates freedom. Not only financial freedom but freedom of time, energy, and attention.

This is where the Simplify Day takes on a deeper role. It becomes more than a productivity tool and starts to function as a leadership discipline. It creates a monthly pause to step back and ask:

- Where am I still the constraint?
- What am I holding onto that no longer serves the business?
- Is our progress accidental or repeatable?
- What does success look like at this stage?

FROM FLEXIBILITY TO FREEDOM

If a truly successful business brings you freedom, how should that freedom look?

I grew up watching my parents experience the flexibility of entrepreneurship. They worked hard, but they had autonomy. They could shape their time and priorities in ways that were not always possible in more traditional paths, and that left a lasting impression on me.

On the surface, that may look like freedom. But what I've learned since is that flexibility without structure eventually collapses. Real freedom is not the absence of responsibility but the presence of clarity. That clarity often comes when you are willing to slow down, reflect, and intentionally design the business instead of constantly reacting to it. That is the kind of freedom worth building toward.

A monthly mechanism to check in, recalibrate, and stay aligned with what matters most is essential to provide the structure for this planning discipline while honoring entrepreneurial independence.

THE IMPORTANCE OF HAVING A TEAM

In the early stages of a business, everything naturally centers on the client. You're scrapping, building, listening, solving, and doing whatever it takes to deliver value and meet real needs. But as the business grows, the work is no longer just about the clients you serve; it's about the people who help you serve them.

Your team becomes the heartbeat of the entire operation. Each person who chooses to work alongside you plays a pivotal role in what your business becomes. Their growth fuels your growth. Their commitment determines your capacity. Their passion shapes the client experience more than you ever could alone. That's why you learn to treat your team as your most important clients because great people deserve great care. When you pour into them, support them, honor the value they bring, and encourage them to think more like owners than employees, they don't just help the business succeed. They help it thrive.

At this stage, the team is the firm. Your team isn't limited to the people on payroll. Your team is your family, your ideal clients, your advocates, your referral partners . . . everyone who believes in your mission and pushes it forward.

When you understand that, you start treating people differently. With more care, more gratitude, more intention. And that shift can become the foundation of a business that grows, endures, and leaves a legacy.

FROM LIFESTYLE BUSINESS TO LEGACY

At a certain level of success, a new choice appears. I like to think of it like a snowball rolling downhill. As it picks up momentum, it gets bigger and moves faster. That's what can happen when you break through from what I'd call a lifestyle business to a growth-minded business.

A lifestyle business supports the owner's life, and that is a great outcome. But when strong teams, excess capacity, and momentum are in place, a different opportunity emerges. You can begin building beyond yourself.

At that point, reinvestment replaces extraction and growth becomes intentional. The business may turn into a platform for opportunity, impact, and long-term value. When the business stops revolving around you, it starts serving something bigger. You can create real career paths for your team. You can build an ownership path where everyone has the opportunity to build some real wealth. That is when abundance shows up, not as excess, but as alignment.

WHAT THIS IS ALL FOR

There's no end to the entrepreneurial journey. There's no final destination where you arrive and everything is complete. The journey continues to change and adapt. And, in my opinion, that's the fun part of it.

The goal was never just to build a profitable business. It was to build a life where success feels aligned, where the business supports who you want to be rather than the other way around.

When you stop reacting, create space to think, and commit to a monthly rhythm of intentional leadership, the business becomes what it was always meant to be. It becomes a platform, a multiplier, and a vehicle for impact. That's what Simplify Day was designed to do, and, in my opinion, that is the real evolution of the entrepreneur.

CONCLUSION:

BREAKING FREE TO ACHIEVE MORE

IMAGINE WAKING UP ON the first Monday of next month knowing exactly what you're going to work on. Not the urgent fires that always find you, but the important work that's been sitting on your list for months. The operating agreement that needs updating. The strategic planning session you keep postponing. The financial review you know you should do but never quite get to.

Now imagine doing this every single month for the next year. Twelve days dedicated entirely to working on your business instead of in it. Twelve opportunities to step back, assess what's working, fix what isn't, and chart the course forward.

The frameworks we've explored throughout this book were designed to help you move in that direction.

But things won't change by simply reading this book.

I can give you every framework, every template, every strategy we use with our most successful clients. But if you close this book and go back to the frenetic rhythm you've been operating in, things are unlikely to improve. You'll still be acting as the quarterback of your team without the proper expertise to do this effectively.

And the difference between those who stay in this rhythm and those who break out of it is execution. But it's important to remember that this execution requires discipline, not perfection. Your first few Simplify Days will probably feel awkward. You won't fill all the time effectively. You'll get distracted . . . and that's normal. What matters is showing up month after month, building the habit, letting the compound effect work. What leads you to a dramatic transformation is consistency.

If you've gotten this far, and you're thinking about how to actually implement all of this, I want you to know you don't have to figure it out alone. At Vance Wealth, we've built our entire team around solving exactly these challenges. We have an in-house CPA who heads our tax planning department, a team of six CFP® professionals, and we've spent years building systems specifically for business owners and entrepreneurs who are tired of trying to be the quarterback without any success.

So, if what you read in this book resonated with you, we can schedule a complimentary discovery call. We'll talk through your specific challenges, what you're dealing with in your business and financial life, and see if how we work might be a good fit.

Now, if you're not quite sure whether you're dealing with these challenges or how significant they might be, we can also perform a complimentary tax assessment. We'll review two years of your tax returns and identify missed opportunities at a high level. If we can show you where you're leaving money on the table with missing tax planning opportunities, that alone might make it worth bringing in proper coordination.

But whether you decide to work with our team or with someone else, just take action on what resonates with you from this book. Maybe it's creating that monthly planning day. Maybe it's having a conversation with your CPA about lifetime tax strategy. Maybe it's finally getting your professional team on the same page. Whatever feels right for where you are, just start there.

Now, as you consider what makes the most sense for your current situation, it can be helpful to recognize that the level of coordination you may need shifts as your income grows and your life becomes more complex.

To help you visualize where you are in this process and the type of guidance you may need, I've included a framework developed from my own experience. It's meant to give you a clearer sense of the stage you may be at and the level of coordination that could be useful at each point.

1

Under $250K
Building the Foundation

YOU are the Quarterback (QB)

- Basic CPA
- Bookkeeper
- Simple advisor
- You coordinate

2

$250K–$500K
Growing Team

You are still the Quarterback (QB)

- More advisors
- More questions
- More decisions
- Feeling stretched

3

$500K–$1M
Rising Complexity

Financial Quarterback (QB) is needed

- Higher stakes
- Tax complexity
- Time crunch
- Missed opportunities

4

$1M+
Full Integration

Financial Quarterback (QB) is essential

- Coordinates team
- Big picture view
- Proactive
- You focus on impact

→ Tiers are based on personal income levels.

Phases 1–2:

You're Managing Everything

You coordinate your team, make all connections, and piece together advice from multiple directions.

Phases 3–4:

Professional Takes the Lead

A Financial Quarterback coordinates your team, spots opportunities, and eliminates friction.

THE REAL QUESTION

Five years from now, you'll be somewhere. The question is whether you'll look back and feel good about the path you took.

Maybe you'll have found ways to step back from the noise and complexity of running a business. Maybe you'll have created more space for the work that matters. Or maybe things will look pretty similar to how they look today. That's not necessarily bad because sometimes staying the course is exactly right.

But the truth is there's no perfect moment to make changes. Next quarter won't be less busy. Next year won't magically have more white space. So the real question is, what's one thing you could do differently that might make the next five years better than the last five?

Small shifts today compound over time, and your future self will be thankful for that.

CONTACT INFORMATION

www.simplify-365.com
www.AugustaRuleinaBox.com
wwwVanceWealth.com

We created simplify365® because being a business owner is complex, and our goal is to simplify your financial life 365 days a year. If we can make every day a little easier, more organized, and more intentional for you, then we're fulfilling the purpose behind this offering

ABOUT THE AUTHOR

JOHN VANCE IS THE founder of Vance Wealth, where he serves as the financial quarterback for over ninety high-earning entrepreneurs and business owners. With over twenty years in the industry, John has built his firm from a startup operation to a thriving practice managing nearly $1 billion in assets with a team of over twenty-five professionals and growing. As a CERTIFIED FINANCIAL PLANNER®, he specializes in helping business owners navigate the financial complexity that comes with entrepreneurial success.

What sets John apart isn't just his credentials. He's lived the exact journey his clients are experiencing. He launched his practice at age twenty-eight, one month before his first daughter was born, with his wife having just left her career to stay home with their newborn. Every solution he offers his clients emerged from a challenge he faced himself and systematized a way through.

Unlike traditional consultants who diagnose problems and leave clients to figure out implementation, John's firm emphasizes execution. His philosophy is that good ideas are everywhere, but the real value lies in getting things done and getting them done right.

At the heart of John's practice is the "Simplify Day" framework, a monthly strategic planning approach he developed for himself and now offers to clients through his simplify365® service. Rather than the traditional once-a-year goal setting,

Simplify Day creates a dedicated monthly checkpoint for business owners to step out of reactive firefighting mode and into strategic thinking. Combined with his lifetime tax philosophy and the Virtual Family Office model, John has built a comprehensive system that addresses the unique challenges of managing wealth when business and personal finances are deeply intertwined.

John's commitment to growth extends beyond his clients. He's been an active member of Vistage, a CEO peer-to-peer group, for over eight years, and participates in Dan Sullivan's Strategic Coach program. He is dedicated to constantly refining his approach and stay ahead of industry changes.

Outside the complex world of business, John lives in Santa Clarita, north of Los Angeles, with his wife and family. Having built a business while raising children and managing his own company's financial challenges, he brings an understanding that goes beyond technical expertise. He knows what it's like when major life events collide with business demands, when there never seem to be enough hours in the day, and when success brings as many challenges as it solves. That personal experience makes him the ideal guide for entrepreneurs who want more than financial advice and those who want a partner who's been exactly where they are and knows the path forward.

www.ingramcontent.com/pod-product-compliance
Lightning Source LLC
LaVergne TN
LVHW022012200926
848481LV00007B/2351